Carlos & Betty

D0027769

Gone but Not Lost

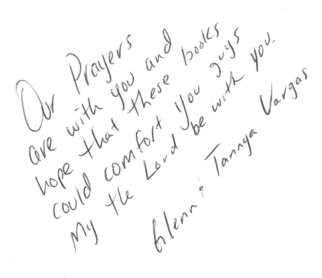
Our Prayers are with you and hope that these books could comfort you guys My the Lord be with you.

Glenn & Tannya Vargas

Gone but Not Lost

Grieving the Death
of a Child

David W. Wiersbe

BAKER BOOK HOUSE
Grand Rapids, Michigan 49516

Copyright © 1992 by Baker Books
a division of Baker Book House Company
P.O. Box 6287, Grand Rapids, MI 49516-6287

ISBN: 0-8010-9716-9

Eleventh printing, May 2003

Printed in the United States of America

For current information about all releases from Baker Book House,
visit our web site:
http://www.bakerbooks.com/

To
Mike and Pat Mulvain

who became my teachers as
they walked through the
valley of the shadow of
death,
and whose lives today
demonstrate that God does
give beauty for ashes, and
the oil of gladness for
mourning

Contents

Preface

$\mathcal{J}$esus always welcomed children into his presence. I believe when a young child dies, he or she enters the presence of Jesus.

Death breaks relationships. Part of the pain and sorrow is still having love to give but our loved one cannot receive it. The assurance and hope Christians have is that those who die in Christ are alive in his presence, and we will be reunited with them one day.

I heard a pastor say in a funeral message, "Our brother is gone from us, but he is not lost. When you know where someone is, they aren't lost. He is in heaven with Jesus. So he is gone from us, but he isn't lost!" This is the assurance and hope that sustains Christian people.

But parents still have to cope with grief, and marriage, and family, and life. This book is to help you better understand what you are experiencing, and to offer help and hope. Jesus Christ, because of his death and resurrection, is the greatest source for information and comfort. God's promises and God's strength will sustain you as you travel through the valley of the shadow of death.

One

The Wounded Parent

In all their affliction
he was afflicted
(Isa. 63:9).

*A*s a bereaved parent you have walked through these experiences: being notified of your child's death; feeling numb; talking with medical people; making arrangements with a funeral director, suddenly being surrounded by visitors, sitting through a service with a sense of unreality, wondering when you will wake up and this will all be over; asking questions that have no answers; constantly feeling pain, and sensing that everyone's life is back to normal but yours.

No one tells us how much death hurts. There is a physical pain beyond describing; some parents have called it "the stomachache that never ends." There is a sense of dislocation, of being on the outside, watching events unfold. But there is also the constant internal awareness that "This is really happening to me, *right now*."

It is not nature's way for a child to die before his or her parents. We expect our parents will precede us in death, then it will be our turn. No parent expects to make his or her child's funeral arrangements.

Children die in so many ways: SIDS (Sudden Infant Death Syndrome), accidents, lingering illnesses, suicide, murder, drug overdose, miscarriage, or stillbirth.

A child can die at any age. It is always a tragedy when a child dies, but it may hurt the eighty-year-old mother just as deeply to lose her fifty-year-old son as it does the mother of a six-year-old.

Pain is part of life—even the pain of grief. The pain of grief is hard to describe, harder to explain, and sometimes overwhelming. It is a special pain, and no drug gives relief. It takes time to come to terms with the pain of grief.

In grief's agonies you are not alone. God cares about what you feel, and what you're going through. God is not indifferent to your pain—he shares it. Consider this affirmation: "In all their affliction he was afflicted, and the angel of his presence saved them" (Isa. 63:9a). When you hurt, God hurts with you and for you. It helps to go to someone who understands how you feel. When you go to God, he promises to comfort and give you strength. Truly he does care and understand like no one else. His Son died too.

Two

A Place Called Heaven:
Questions Parents Ask

I shall go to him,
but he shall not return to me
(2 Sam. 12:23a).

$\mathcal{W}$here do children go when they die? The Bible tells us they go to heaven, into the presence of God.

King David had an infant son who died when he was seven days old. David's response indicates he believed his son was somewhere David would also go. That somewhere is *heaven*.

A child belongs in his or her parents' arms. That's how it should be. No other place could be better or safer; or so we feel.

When someone dies, the soul leaves the body. Our bodies are "tents"—the houses the "real us" live in. Paul wrote that when we are away from the body, we are at home with the Lord (2 Cor. 5:8). Paul also seems to indicate that when Christians die, the Lord Jesus comes and puts them to sleep, and they awake in glory (1 Thess. 4:14). "Sleep" is one of the most common pictures for death in the New Testament. We don't fear sleep; it's something we need.

The person who dies isn't asleep. He or she is alive and alert in the presence of God! Heaven is a place of perfection, so it's possible that children don't stay children there. They may grow up. Heaven is a place where no desire goes unsatisfied, where there is no pain. In heaven there is complete understanding. All questions are answered. Heaven is a place of joy, safety, and love.

But we aren't in heaven yet. We hurt. We have questions, but we also have a promise from Jesus: "Father, I want those you have given me to be with me where I am, and to see my glory" (John 17:24a NIV). One day Jesus will gather all his followers to himself, and there will be a glorious reunion. This is what King David meant when he said of his infant son, "I will go to him."

Jesus is the way to heaven: "I am the way, the truth, and the life" (John 14:6a). Those who believe Jesus died for their sins on the cross, and rose again, go to heaven when they die. Those too young to hear and understand that story enter heaven too, because God is just and gracious. He will not condemn a person who never had a chance to hear and believe. Jesus, who always welcomed children, has a place reserved for them in his presence.

Questions Parents Ask

1. *Our loss was a miscarriage. Do we have a child in heaven?*
   The Bible teaches that from the moment of conception we are persons in the eyes of God (Jer. 1:5; Ps. 139:13–16). The developing, unborn child is a unique person. When the

process of development ends, that child's soul enters paradise.

2. *Our son was never baptized. Does this mean he is not in heaven?*

   Baptism is an important Christian rite, but baptism does not save: Jesus does. The thief who was being crucified next to Jesus believed, but was never baptized. Yet Jesus promised the man he would be in paradise that day (Luke 23:42–43). God is love. He is not going to keep a child out of heaven for something that child could not control. Salvation and heaven are gifts God gives us through Jesus.

3. *Is my child an angel?*

   No. Saved human beings are higher than the angels. Angels are the ministers of God who do his bidding. But people have the most intimate relationship with God. God actually became a man in the person of Jesus to save us. When we enter heaven, we become like Jesus: He "will transform our lowly bodies so that they will be like his glorious body" (Phil. 3:21b NIV).

4. *Will I know my child in heaven? Will he or she know me?*

   Yes. The Scripture indicates that in heaven people recognize each other. Because heaven is a place of perfection, those who died as infants or children will probably be grown up. We will know them.

5. *Does my son know how much I love and miss him?* I believe that God tells our loved ones in glory the things they need to know. Those in heaven are no longer concerned primarily with events on earth, yet what occurred on earth during our lifetime matters in heaven. Those in heaven understand the events of their earthly life, and are at peace about them. Most importantly, *God* knows how much we love and miss the child who died, and he gives comfort and strength.

Three

Out of the Depths

*Out of the depths
have I cried unto you, O LORD.
LORD, hear my voice
(Ps. 130:1–2a).*

*I*t feels like drowning. You're in water over your head, can't catch your breath. Going deeper and deeper. It's the depths—the depths of grief and sorrow.

The depths are a confusing place to be. It's hard to tell what is real. You go through the motions of living but don't feel you're alive. Life is out of sync, dislocated. Sometimes in the depths you think about how much better it would be if life were over.

But God is with you in the depths. The depths are what Jesus experienced on the cross. They aren't where you want to be, but you aren't there alone. Nothing can separate you from God (Rom. 8:38–39)—not even death.

We learn some lessons in the depths we can't learn anywhere else. We learn to live by faith. A child's death makes us realize how little control we have in life. Trusting God is the only way to survive.

We learn to wait. Life can be lived only a breath at a time, an hour at a time, a day at a time. The depths slow us down and make us think about what truly matters. By waiting we get to know God. "Those who wait on the Lord will gain new strength" (see Isa. 40:31).

We also learn to hope. Death will not be reversed. We know that. Hope is not "wishful thinking." It is confident expectation that God will fulfill his promises. He promises to see us *through* (Isa. 43:2). He promises reunion with those who have entered glory ahead of us (John 17:24). He promises to meet today's needs. He promises that life will begin again.

The question is "*How* will you go through the depths?" Put your trust in God—*now*.

four

Part of You Is Gone

Woe is me for my hurt!
my wound is grievous:
but I said, Truly this is a grief,
and I must bear it
(Jer. 10:19).

When your car breaks down, you go to a mechanic. He puts in new parts, makes adjustments, and the car runs fine. If your body is ill, the doctor examines you, and makes a diagnosis. Perhaps medicine or surgery can cure the problem. With treatment you're healthy again.

Those models don't work when it comes to grief. Part of you, part of your life, died when your child died. That part of you is irreplaceable. There are no interchangeable parts to get you through grief. You have to adjust.

Think of grief as a kind of rehabilitation. When people lose their eyesight, there are ways of coping. Blind persons can learn Braille, get a Seeing Eye dog, and learn to use a cane. When hearing is lost, there are hearing aids, sign language, and lip reading. Living through the aftershock of death teaches you new ways to cope and survive. Life is never the same after a loved one dies. You have to learn new ways of thinking, feeling, and acting.

Life is still worth living, but first there are adjustments to make. They aren't easy: missing a face at the dinner table; not tucking in son or daughter at bedtime; fewer Christmas presents to buy; tears coming at surprising moments. But you *can* make these adjustments as you walk through the grieving process. Determine that you will survive.

You'll never forget your child. Life won't be the same. You can hang onto God as you go through the changes, because he doesn't change. "Jesus Christ the same yesterday, to day, and for ever" (Heb. 13:8). His love surrounds you. His strength is in you, and he will help you to face each new day.

Five

The Grieving Process

My soul refused to be comforted
(Ps. 77:2c).

They that wait upon the LORD
shall renew their strength
(Isa. 40:31a).

*A*n acorn planted in fertile soil requires sun and rain—and many years—to become a tall oak tree. Growing from seed to mature tree takes T-I-M-E. Grief is a process, and it takes time. You will not "get over" your sorrow today or next month. Grieving cannot be hurried. Grief is also work—it demands concentration and choices.

Each person grieves differently. We walk through the stages of our sorrow in different orders. What follows is a brief summary of some of the experiences you can expect as you grieve the death of your child. You probably won't experience them in the order they are presented. Knowing what you're experiencing will affirm that you are *normal*—all grieving people feel these emotions and think these things.

Grief begins with *shock,* like being punched in the stomach so the wind is knocked out of you. There is a numbness and inability to feel. Many times the funeral is over before the numbness wears off.

"I'll wake up soon, and find out this is all a bad dream" is one way of expressing *denial.* It's hard to believe this is really happening to *you.* Many grieving people try to bargain with God at this point: "I'll do anything to get my child back." But nothing can bring that precious child back.

For some *tears* come right away. Others take time to be able to cry. Grief needs expression, and crying is one way for us to release our anguish. The need to cry can last a long time.

"Someone's going to pay for this!" is a sign of *anger*. We feel there ought to be someone to blame. Some parents blame themselves, some blame God. Being angry is normal, but anger needs to be channeled in constructive—not destructive—ways.

The feeling that you're drowning, overwhelmed by all the emotions and decisions and pain, can lead to *despair*. "I just don't feel as though I can keep going" is what grieving people say. That *is* how they feel, but they keep going in spite of the feelings.

Confusion feels like a hurricane is snatching you up, spinning you around, destroying your connections with life. Some mourners think about suicide. Others have difficulty with relationships. This is when parents in the grieving process ask, "Am I going crazy?" The answer is *no*. This is how grief feels at this point. Because you have probably never felt this way before, you don't recognize this as part of your sorrow. It's unpleasant; it's also normal.

Every mourner tastes *depression*. It is bitter. Being down, burdened, withdrawing from family or friends are evidences of being depressed. Grief produces depression; it's part of how individuals respond to loss. Being with people is good though, and so is doing something for yourself. Depression will come; you don't have to give it a permanent address.

When you begin to see a ray of light in your dungeon of darkness, it means you are starting to *hope.* Hope means looking ahead and not only behind. The ability to laugh, to enjoy a sunrise, a beautiful rose, or a good meal, means you're realizing life has not come to an end.

One afternoon Judy called her daughter's pediatrician. "Doctor Peterson, I'm calling to thank you for all you did for Nicole before she died. If you have time, I'd like you to explain her disease to me again." For Judy, that conversation indicated she was coming to terms with her child's death. *Acceptance* comes only with time, but when you can say "I'm ready to hear the truth," acceptance has arrived.

When you find yourself ready for a new venture in your life, it is the harbinger of a *new beginning.* The wounds may not all be healed, and the scars may be tender, but you're ready to start a new chapter in life. You have suffered a severe loss. When a person loses her hearing, she learns to use sign language. In grieving, you learn new skills to help you live. Attempting something new is a sign your rehabilitation process is nearing an end.

Remember, not everyone goes through each of these "stages." You may cycle through some experiences several times. There is no "right" order. There is also no magic time limit when you suddenly have completed grieving. Each person moves through grief at his or her own pace. You will know inside when the process is almost over. Grief is a process, and it takes *time*. Give yourself permission to grieve.

Six

Grief Is Not Rational

*Why is my pain perpetual,
and my wound incurable?
(Jer. 15:18a).*

*P*erhaps the most direct way to say it," she said with a serious face, "is that I think I'm going crazy. I feel out of touch. I feel like I'm losing it." The speaker was a mother whose teenager had died three months earlier. She looked good and dressed fashionably. She was holding down her job, and holding her home together. To all appearances her transition through the grief process was going smoothly.

But she was struggling. Sometimes this mom was angry: other times tears came unbidden, and she was embarrassed. She knew God loved her, but she also wrestled with how a loving God could allow her child to die, just as her life was blossoming.

Grief is not rational. All the logic in the world will not allow you to escape the ache inside. It is an emotional jumble. The feelings are real: the mental and physical pain; the sense that it's all a dream and you'll wake soon; the denial; the caldron of boiling anger, the confusion; embarrassment of one's emotions; disappointment, and frustration.

All these feelings (and others you've had) are normal during the grieving process. The fact that you feel and think these things says that you are *healthy!* You're experiencing what others have tasted in their walk through the valley of sorrow. You are not alone.

In some ways those in sorrow are the healthiest people in town. They know they hurt. They express their feelings. They cry. They ask the tough questions they know no one can fully answer. They get mad and say angry words. For those in grief, this is normal. It shows their minds and feelings and bodies are functioning in healthy ways.

Seven

The Tears of God

Jesus wept
(John 11:35).

God shall wipe away
all tears from their eyes
(Rev. 7:17c).

When Jesus' friend Lazarus died, Jesus was away. When Jesus reached the grave four days later, he stood by the tomb and wept. God the Son shed tears over his friend taken by death.

What do we learn from the fact that Jesus cried?

Tears are natural. We are made with the ability to cry when we hurt. It is our body's way of releasing grief and tension. We'll cry many, many tears in our times of grief. God notes every tear we shed (Ps. 56:8).

Tears are a sign of love. Jesus loved Lazarus, and was deeply moved at the fact of his death. I believe Jesus was angry at the pain death inflicted on the people he loved. You weep and sob because you love your child. You don't stop loving when someone dies.

Tears are a sign of strength. Our culture tells us men shouldn't cry; we think it looks weak. Jesus was a strong man, physically and spiritually, and Lazarus' death made him cry. Tears say we can respond normally (with tears) to an abnormal situation (death). People who can cry are demonstrating emotional and spiritual health.

Grief is a time for tears and crying without feeling embarrassed or ashamed. The tears need to come—they're part of *good* grief. One day the God who sees each tear that falls will wipe every tear away.

Eight

Styles of Grieving

I set my face like a flint
(Isa. 50:7b).

Rachel [was] weeping
for her children,
and would not be comforted
(Matt. 2:18b).

Some people can express their sorrow easily and openly. Shedding tears is a necessary, healthy way of showing grief. So is asking questions, and feeling angry. Often sorrow removes our appetite, and food loses its taste (It is still important to eat!). Some parents can reminisce about their son or daughter, and laugh or cry without hesitation. But others have a difficult time showing their feelings.

Each of us is made differently. For some personalities, it is almost impossible to cry publicly, or even talk about deep, personal feelings. These people need to grieve privately: to weep, talk about their loss, to reminisce. What is most important is that each parent whose child has died express his or her grief in some way.

When a wife can grieve openly, but her husband is private about his grief, problems can arise. For instance, the wife may think her husband doesn't care about what happened, that he has no feelings. Of course that's not true. But the husband may think his wife is over-reacting, crying all the time and not dealing with reality. He may well be wrong.

Grieving is an individual process, and no two people go through it in the same way or at the same rate. A husband may express his grief through anger or withdrawal, while his wife may be starting to accept what has happened. A wife may withdraw from her circle of friends and relationships, while her husband seeks people out. One spouse may quietly go through the family photo albums at home, while the other regularly mentions the deceased child in conversation with friends. Work can become an unhealthy escape from the situation. Tears can become a way to avoid responsibilities that should be resumed.

To survive, spouses have to talk to each other about their grief. They share a common loss, but also experience it individually. Discussing what each one is feeling and thinking will keep husband and wife from making faulty assumptions and reaching wrong conclusions.

Betty was energetic and intense, and her grieving style was quite open. She cried when she needed to, talked about her feelings, and showed pictures of her daughter Shelly to folks she talked to. Dan, her husband, returned to his usual routine a week after their daughter's death. Betty never saw him cry, and when she talked about Shelly, he listened and then changed the subject.

Because Dan's response differed from hers, Betty assumed Dan didn't love Shelly, and was just "cold." One day she came home early from work and found

Dan in the bedroom, looking at Shelly's baby book and sobbing. The walls Betty had begun building crumbled. She realized it was a mistake to assume Dan would grieve as she did. After that, Betty and Dan made a point to talk regularly about how they were adjusting.

Of course, some people don't like to talk about how they feel. This is where a pastor or close friend needs to assist a couple in keeping the lines of communication open. Talking gets the pain and frustration out of the dark, into the light. Then healing can begin. We cannot deal with what we cannot name. Discussing thoughts and feelings helps us "name" what bothers us, and moves us toward solutions.

It is a tremendous comfort to learn another person feels what you feel. It may not be felt in the same way, but you are helped when you know you are not alone in your suffering.

Nine

Facts and Feelings

The LORD gave,
and the LORD has taken away;
blessed be the name of the LORD
(Job 1:21b).

O that my grief
were thoroughly weighed
(Job 6:2a).

The facts are there all the time, hammering at you. He died, a victim of disease. She died in the accident. My child is dead, gone. I am a mourner, a pilgrim on the path of sorrow.

The feelings are there, too. Empty arms ache to hug and cuddle the child again. Eyes burn from too many tears. Stomachache, headache. Wishing it weren't true, wanting to be alone, wanting not to be alone. It's an emotional muddle, and you're in the middle.

You may feel God hates you. Or that he is punishing you for something you did long ago. You may feel God is far away, and has forgotten you. You may feel wrathful against God, or hate him. Those feelings, too, are part of grief.

At times a peace may steal over you, but it doesn't last as long as you'd like. The emptiness commands attention, and tears flow again.

Human beings feel a lot of emotions, all at the same time. Grief forces us to accept that we are human. Human beings cry and ache when someone they love deeply has died. We are complex creatures, and can't always understand what we are doing, or why we feel as we do.

Keep this truth in mind: *Feelings are real, but feelings are not necessarily reality.* For instance, you may feel God is punishing you, but in fact God loves you. And God loves you even though you feel he doesn't. Maybe you feel life is no longer worth living; but you still have much to live for, and people who need you. It is difficult to bring how you feel into line with what you know. But it's important to you, and your family, that you try.

In the story of the man named Job, a series of disasters wiped out everything he had in a single day. A major part of Job's grief was the death of his seven children. He wept, and was angry, and argued with his friends and with his God. But through his experience, he never forgot the facts. He knew he'd been faithful to God, and he knew God would be faithful to him. He believed God was listening and that God cared. He knew God would support and help him. Job walked through the emotions of grief. But he based his decisions on the facts, and not on how he felt. Feelings will change; God will not change; *God's promises will not change.*

Ten

The Mourner's Creed

When I am weak,
then am I strong
(2 Cor. 12:10b).

I can do all things
through Christ which strengtheneth me
(Phil. 4:13).

*I*n grief God seems to have abandoned us. He hasn't. In grief we feel as if nothing matters. It does. Sometimes we think life is not worth living; it is! In times of sorrow people of faith have to "believe against the grain." In our weakness, God reveals his strength, and we do more than we thought possible.

Faith means clinging to God in spite of circumstances. It means following him when we cannot see, being faithful to him when we don't feel like it.

Mourners need a creed; it is "I believe!" We need to affirm this creed daily:

I believe God's promises are true.
I believe heaven is real.
I believe I will see my child again.
I believe God will see me through.
I believe nothing can separate me from God's love.
I believe God has work for me to do.

"Believing against the grain" means having a survivalist attitude. Bereaved parents are survivors; they have endured. Not only do they survive, but also out of grief they create something good. Your attitude toward grieving determines if the outcome is health or sickness.

Before his son was killed, Pete was a hard, silent man. He didn't let anyone know what was inside him. He kept his feelings and thoughts to himself. In the months after his son's death, Pete was transformed. He cried in public. He talked about his feelings. He hugged his family, much to their surprise. He went out of his way to meet other bereaved parents and encourage them. In time Pete's life was marked by love and laughter and openness. His son's death showed him how important it was to live, how important people are.

Grieving is not easy work—but it is necessary work. Build on these foundation stones:

I will believe in God.
I will survive.
I will turn my grief to good, somehow.
I will enjoy life.
I will contribute to the good of others.

You may feel you're swimming upstream, believing against the grain. Remember: attitude determines outcome. Living by faith works!

Eleven

The Marital Strain

Two are better than one. . . .
If they fall, the one will lift up the other.
But woe to him that is alone
when he falls—
he has no one to help him up
(see Eccles. 4:9–10).

Love suffers long, and is kind. . . .
Love bears all things,
believes all things,
hopes all things,
endures all things.
Love never fails
(see 1 Cor. 13:4, 7, 8a).

*T*here is a domino effect in families where a child dies. It's as if crisis begets crisis. Husband and wife experience stress in their marriage. Parents and remaining children have conflict. Bereaved parents may have problems with their parents (the grandparents of the child who died).

Think of your life as a huge ball of yarn with many strands of many different colors. Each colored strand represents one of the people you know and love. When one of them dies, the entire ball of yarn has to be unwound to remove the single strand. That's how it feels when a family member dies. Your life is "unwound," and that creates tension and conflict.

Conflict in a marriage and home after a child has died is normal. Each person grieves in his or her own way, and progresses through grief at an individual pace. If conflict is recognized and handled appropriately, healing will take place. If not, damage can be done.

Husbands and wives especially struggle in the aftermath of the death and funeral. Divorce rates for bereaved couples are extremely high. Many couples report sexual problems, emotional distance, and more fighting than before. If the child was the glue that held the marriage together, the couple has to find a new foundation for their relationship.

These bad results don't have to happen. Here are some suggestions to help resolve the differences and conflicts that can arise.

1. Remember that each person grieves differently.
2. Support your spouse physically, emotionally, spiritually.
3. Take the time to talk about your thoughts and feelings with your spouse.
4. Give each other permission to grieve openly.
5. Concentrate on *resolving* conflicts, instead of on the conflicts themselves.
6. Do things together: quiet walks, going to church, praying, going through the cards people sent, dining out.
7. Focus on the future.

Some couples are afraid of sex after a child has died, because of the possibility of pregnancy. There's a danger in thinking another child can be a "replacement." But each child is a unique individual—irreplaceable. You need physical intimacy in grief. When both partners agree to it, lovemaking can provide affirmation and comfort. If nothing else, at least talk about sex, and where it fits as a priority in your marriage now.

After God made the first man, he said "It is not good for the man to be alone" (Gen. 2:18a). Then God made Eve for Adam. It is never good for humans to be alone, especially in time of sorrow. Grief can bring a husband and wife closer together than ever before, if you decide it will be that way.

After their son died, Mark and Pam decided that they would live in such a way that good things would grow out of their loss. They made investing in their marriage a priority. They went to church together, and joined a support group together. Pam and Mark built a strong relationship because they worked through their sorrow as a team.

Twelve

Needing to Know

Now I know in part;
but then shall I know fully
(1 Cor. 13:12b NIV).

*C*urt needed to know the details of the accident that took his son's life. He interviewed witnesses, examined police reports, and asked many questions of the funeral director.

Susan questioned her daughter's doctors constantly, trying to understand the sudden death. She read dozens of books, and even called other families who had gone through the same experience.

Some parents need to know as much about what took their son or daughter as they can learn. Knowing gives them a measure of peace. If that's you, that's okay. Direct as many questions as you need to, to the right people. Most doctors, nurses, police officers, paramedics, and funeral directors are happy to take the time to answer you.

But other parents just don't want to know. Giving them more information than they require can be unfair and painful. Grief is easier for them by knowing less.

"Do you want to know about this?" is a good question to ask before you reveal details about the death, or funeral arrangements, or medical facts. And if you're the one being told, retain your right to be treated with respect. If the conversation makes you uncomfortable, say, "I would rather not hear about this, please."

You have the right to choose whether or not to know the details. And others should respect your decision. Neither choice is wrong; make the one right for you.

Thirteen

Guilt

But there is forgiveness with thee
(Ps. 130:4a).

*I*f only I'd called the doctor sooner." "What if we'd stayed home that day?" "Did we try everything possible to save her life?" "Did he look both ways before crossing the road?" "I should have known something was wrong!" "If only I had used other words."

Those comments—and many more like them—come from the minds and lips of bereaved parents. A weight presses on your mind and heart, becoming a personal burden of guilt about your child's death.

When something goes wrong, people assume there has to be someone to blame. Many parents realize their child's death was no one's *fault;* yet they feel guilty and blame themselves. Guilt, someone said, is anger turned in on ourselves.

It is normal to feel some guilt. It's hard to believe circumstances can be so far beyond your control. Insisting on taking responsibility for a situation you could not change is not healthy. Blaming yourself will not bring healing, only deeper wounds. Self-inflicted punishment is not good grief.

Maybe you had an argument with your son before he died, or you said things you want to take back. Guilt for those kinds of experiences may be right. And there is relief from the guilt: confess what you did to God. He will forgive you. Your child in heaven already understands and forgives too. No one holds a grudge in heaven. God forgives you; you must forgive yourself.

Fourteen

Mad at God

But it displeased Jonah exceedingly,
and he was very angry
(Jon. 4:1).

*E*ven if God didn't cause my child's death, he certainly allowed it!" said an angry parent at a meeting. Many heads nodded at his words, affirming that other parents felt the same.

Anger can be aimed in many directions. Some grievers take it out on their spouse or boss. Others vent their frustration on the doctors and nurses, or the funeral director, or the pastor. The child who died can be a target for anger, too.

When we're angry, God is a convenient target. He doesn't hit back. Lots of people have been angry with God, and God has always been big enough to take it.

Anger is hostility aroused by a sense of being wronged (whether the wrong is real or perceived). A child's death is wrong—and it results in anger.

Anger is an honest emotion that needs expression. Suppressed anger can become headaches, stomach problems, heart attack, or a stroke. But it's hard to admit being mad at *God.* After all, he's in charge. We fear that his response to our anger will be to judge us or just ignore us. Our fears are unfounded.

Anger is like fire: If it is properly harnessed, it can do much good. If it is left to burn uncontrolled, it can do only damage. Decide that when you are angry, you will use the anger constructively.

Talk about how you feel—admit that you are angry. Admitting it gives you the freedom to examine why you feel it. Trying to hide anger never works; it always surfaces. Holding it in only guarantees an explosion one day.

Perhaps you are angry about what your child's death denies you—all the good experiences of seeing a little one grow to maturity. You feel cheated. Maybe your child was killed by a drunk driver. Maybe it's the not knowing that makes you angry.

Once the source of anger is identified, there are actions you can take to diminish anger's power. You can work against alcoholism. You can pray about your feelings of helplessness at not understanding why your child died. You can talk to other bereaved parents about your feelings and discover what they have learned. You may contribute to healing their wounds.

If it's a person you're angry at, you may need to talk with him or her. Not to inflict pain on them, but to forgive them. Forgiveness has a way of extinguishing anger's fire. It is not easy to forgive, but by God's grace, you can.

Don't hide your anger from yourself or God. Face it honestly, and it won't control your life.

Fifteen

Going Through

When thou passest through the waters,
I will be with thee; and through the rivers,
they shall not overflow thee.
When thou walkest through the fire,
thou shalt not be burned;
neither shall the flame kindle upon thee
(Isa. 43:2).

*T*he key word in this verse is *through*. God promises you will get *through* the waters of grief, the river of sorrow, the furnace of pain. Somehow you will get *through*. What you experience today will not last forever.

One encouragement here is God knows who you are. He is your Creator, and he calls you by name (Isa. 43:1). You are his, and he will take care of his own. In time of sorrow you feel unimportant and unknown. God knows you, and you are important to him.

God also knows where you are. He knows when you're fighting the current of the river of sorrow, when you're walking through the fiery furnace of suffering. Others may not know what you're experiencing. On the outside you may have everyone believing you're fine. But inside you're about to drown. God knows—and he is there with you.

When Daniel's three friends were thrown into the furnace, the king watched (Dan. 3:22–26). And what he saw amazed him: the men were not harmed, and a fourth person was with them in the furnace. It was Jesus!

God knows how you feel: alone, afraid, uncertain about the future, isolated, maybe rejected. God made you with your emotions, and he knows how they can overwhelm and control you. God will never condemn you for the way you feel. Tell him how it feels—he will listen.

God knows what you need. You need someone to share the pain, to walk through this long valley with you. He promises his presence: "I will be with you." He also promises his love: "'You are precious and honored in my sight, and . . . I love you'" (Isa. 43:4a NIV). God gave you his Son to conquer death and give hope.

Live on promises, not on explanations. Even if God explained why your child died, the answer wouldn't end the heartbreak or quench the questions. Instead of explanations, God gives promises, which keep you moving ahead, giving hope and new strength.

You'll get through your grief. It won't end today or next month. But there is an end. Just face today. Tomorrow will take care of itself. Don't burn today's energies on tomorrow's problems that aren't here yet.

You're going to make it *through*.

Sixteen

Questions

My God, my God, why . . . ?
(Mark 15:34a).

Master, carest thou not that we perish?
(Mark 4:38b).

*I*t's normal and necessary for grieving people to ask questions. The only "dumb" question is the one you don't ask. Don't be afraid of what people will think. You want to know, and the question burns within, so *ask*.

There are some questions bereaved parents ask that have no answers. At least there's no one on earth who can provide a satisfactory solution. Many of your most difficult questions include God. For people with a deep faith, the questions are especially difficult:

> How can a loving God allow something awful like this?
> I've been faithful. Where is God now that I need him?
> Why *my* son/daughter?
> Why did this have to happen *now*?
> How can this possibly be "God's will"?
> I hurt so badly; doesn't God care about me?
> Am I being punished for some previous sin?
> I'm really mad at God—will he hate me now?
> How strong does God think I am?

Many hurting people asked similar questions in Scripture. They did not always receive answers. Job threw all sorts of questions at God; in the end, what he got was more questions (Job 38)! Even Jesus on the cross asked God, "Why?"

Asking these questions is an evidence of faith. If you didn't believe in God, you wouldn't waste your time questioning him. But you do believe—and so you question God.

Receiving detailed answers to your questions would not relieve the pain. Even with a full explanation, life would still require major adjustments. Rarely does God explain himself. But he does give you his promises. (See the next chapter.)

Some of your friends may try to answer your questions. Beware of people who have all the answers! Sometimes grievers ask the questions because it's a way of expressing how they feel. They don't expect a full response.

When you ask the tough questions, it is evidence you take God and your faith seriously. God knows your need to make sense of life. He hears your questions; he sees your tears. Promises are his response.

Seventeen

The Rope of Hope

There hath not failed one word
of all his good promise
(1 Kings 8:56b).

*J*ust as a mountain climber relies on a rope for support and protection, those who mourn rely on God's promises. God's words, spoken to us in time of need, give us the ability to "hang on." Here is a brief collection of promises for those who mourn. These are promises for you to claim, whenever you need them.

In all their distress he too was distressed,
and the angel of his presence saved them.
In his love and mercy he redeemed them;
he lifted them up and carried them
all the days of old (Isa. 63:9 NIV).

The Lord is my shepherd (Ps. 23:1a).

For God so loved the world that he gave his one and only Son, that whoever believes in him shall not perish but have eternal life (John 3:16 NIV).

I am the resurrection and the life. He who believes in me will live, even though he dies; and whoever lives and believes in me will never die (John 11:25–26 NIV).

God will wipe away every tear from their eyes (Rev. 7:17a NIV).

He who goes out weeping,
carrying seed to sow,
will return with songs of joy,
carrying sheaves with him (Ps. 126:6 NIV).

Blessed are those who mourn, for they shall be comforted (Matt. 5:4).

Come to me, all you who are weary and burdened, and I will give you rest (Matt. 11:28 NIV).

Praise be to the God and Father of our Lord Jesus Christ, the Father of compassion and the God of all comfort, who comforts us in all our troubles (2 Cor. 1:3–4a NIV).

When you pass through the waters,
I will be with you;
and when you pass through the rivers,
they will not sweep over you.
When you walk through the fire,
you will not be burned;
the flames will not set you ablaze (Isa. 43:2 NIV).

The Spirit helps us in our weakness. We do not know how we ought to pray, but the Spirit himself intercedes for us with groans that words cannot express (Rom. 8:26 NIV).

For I am convinced that neither death nor life, neither angels nor demons, neither the present nor the future, nor any powers, neither height nor depth, nor anything else in all creation, will be able to separate us from the love of God that is in Christ Jesus our Lord (Rom. 8:38–39 NIV).

My grace is sufficient for you, for my power is made perfect in weakness (2 Cor. 12:9).

Eighteen

Mary
the Mother of Jesus

*There stood by the cross of Jesus
his mother
(John 19:25a).*

*H*e was born in difficult circumstances, but she loved him. His stepfather died while he was a boy, and being a single parent took its toll on her. But she raised a fine boy to be a man.

When he went out on his own, she worried. But everyone seemed to like him, and he was popular. She relaxed. Then people began talking against him—*important* people.

He was accused of crimes he didn't commit, of statements he did not make. In a mockery of justice, they sentenced him to death. She saw him shamefully executed. The child she carried all those months, the little boy who played around the house, the man who carried on the family carpentry business—she saw him die.

The *Pieta* (the statue of Mary, holding the crucified Jesus) reminds us of the agony of the mother of Jesus. "Is any suffering like my suffering?" (Lam. 1:12b NIV). Grieving parents can identify with her.

Mary's tears fell at the foot of the cross. Her heart was broken, her dreams shattered. "A sword will pierce your own soul" the prophet had said (Luke 2:35b NIV). She knew the awful pain. And still—she believed. What God had promised about her son's birth came true; God would still be faithful.

And he was! God raised Jesus from the dead. His resurrection is our source of hope and strength. Because Jesus died and rose, death is not the end. There is the promise of reunion in his presence one day. And Jesus returned to life, affirming that life is worth living.

Nineteen

Preserving the Memories

Can a woman forget
her . . . child?
(Isa. 49:15a).

$\mathcal{Y}$our child's death does not erase the fact that he or she lived. It is a natural instinct to want to preserve the memories you and your family have. But it needs to be done in healthy ways that allow you and your family to grow and change while remembering.

Mary and Paul wanted a memorial for their daughter that would bring joy and beauty to other people, the way Julie did. They finally decided to plant a special tree in a nearby park. They worked with the local park district to make the arrangements. The dedication service was beautiful, attended by family and many of Julie's friends. A friend read a poem written for the occasion, Mary said a few words, and another friend offered a prayer. A plaque was installed near the tree, explaining the tree's special purpose.

Some families establish a memorial fund in the name of the child who died. The monies are then used for charitable purposes, and the family knows that good is being done in their child's memory. The pediatric unit of a hospital, or a local Rescue Squad, is an appropriate recipient of such funds.

Tommy loved going to Sunday school. He looked forward to being with his teacher and friends each week. After he died, Tommy's parents made a donation to the church, to refurnish the department Tommy belonged to. A plaque was hung in Tommy's classroom, to preserve Tommy's memory, but also to indicate his influence lived on.

It is good to remember your child's birthday. You may not want to celebrate, but reminiscing about the birth, and other birthdays, will help bring healing. Visiting the cemetery helps some families too, as long as they remember the child is in heaven. Telling stories about the child who is gone, but not lost, is important at family gatherings. It affirms this person was part of your lives, and helped to shape who you are.

Photographs provide an excellent record of your child and family. A family picture on the wall keeps the memory alive. Some families make a special photo album, or scrapbook, and keep it handy. Looking at pictures of your child, or drawings and letters, can be a source of healing.

The day of your child's death is not a happy anniversary. Some families try to ignore it. But others have a memorial prayer service on that day, or do something special for other people in the child's name.

Choose ways of remembering that are comfortable for you. Think about happy times you had together and the child's personal triumphs and joyous times. You might also recall some humorous occasions. Don't worry, you won't ever forget the child you love. By keeping his or her memory alive, you ease your own grief and can minister to others.

Twenty

Resistance and Acceptance

*How often would I have gathered
thy children together . . .
and ye would not!
(Luke 13:34b).*

A wounded person instinctively withdraws from others. Solitude seems preferable to society. There are no looks to avoid, no words to say, no questions to answer, no tears to hide. "Why don't you just leave me alone?" is a question every mourning person asks.

And yet, even though you feel like being alone, what you really need is to be in the presence of people. You're not your normal self; you're not healthy. But talk and tears are good therapy.

Grief is something deep inside you, and for healing to take place, the grief has to come *out*. One of the best ways for grief to come out is by being with others who understand what you are going through.

Many groups exist for grieving parents. (A list of such groups is in the Appendix.) Each person who attends knows what it is to have a child die. Meetings are led by sensitive survivors of loss, grief, and healing. People at every stage of the grieving process attend the meetings and find help.

A support group is safe. You don't have to talk if you don't want to. Tears are common. Feelings are accepted. No judgments are passed. No one has all the answers.

Being with others who admit their loss helps you to accept your own loss. Saying, "My son was killed in a car accident," helps you to face reality.

It is good to discover that your thoughts and feelings are not yours alone. A support group gives reassurance: what you're going through is normal for a grieving parent. That lesson cannot be learned in isolation.

Other parents in the group become a source of wisdom. They know how to respond to situations you're facing. They know the right words to say. They give genuine encouragement because they have survived.

Many churches offer workshops or support groups for people who are grieving. If you aren't ready to face a group, talk with your pastor. Most pastors are quite willing to attend a support group meeting with members of their church family. Or ask a relative, a friend, or another church member to attend with you. This person will benefit from the experience. It's not so unnerving if you go with someone else.

Your instincts will resist invitations to be with others. If you accept that you *need* time with others who share your path, a support group can become a place for healing.

Twenty-one

Circle of Love, Circle of Grief

Weep with them that weep
(Rom. 12:15b).

Grieving persons tend to focus on *their* feelings, *their* needs, *their* day. This is normal; there isn't much energy to invest in others.

But when a child dies, the entire circle of family and friends is affected. Not only are there bereaved parents; there are bereaved grandparents, bereaved siblings, and friends. It's easy to forget how large the circle of grief is. It is good to discover you are not alone in your sorrow.

Each person affected by your child's death will grieve differently. For grandparents, the death of a grandchild is an unnatural thing. It may increase their sense of mortality.

Bereaved siblings urgently need their parents, and will continue to make the usual demands. For the entire family, it is important to keep living. Resist the temptation to withdraw from life. Let your children continue in Little League or gymnastics. If your family regularly went out for dinner on Friday night, stick to the routine.

When family and friends are together, talk about your feelings. Reminisce about the child who died. Laugh and cry together. This will allow everyone to grieve in healthy ways, and keep the bonds of love strong. When a family member needs time alone to grieve, give space and silence. Make sure that person remains part of the group, though.

Twenty-two

A Ready Response

*A word fitly spoken is like apples of gold
in pictures of silver
(Prov. 25:11).*

One of the sensitive situations you will face is responding to people who raise the fact of your child's death. Most people who do this do not intend to add to your pain, but questions and statements will come, and you need to be ready to answer in a way that allows you to control the conversation. Good responses indicate that you have suffered a loss, the topic is open for discussion, but you set the limits to the conversation.

"Do you have children?" is a common conversation starter. For a bereaved parent, it can also be a tear starter. For parents who have had miscarriages, one response is "We have a child in heaven."

"Do you have only one child?" is more difficult to answer. Why do other people make your family life their business? One mother at a Bereaved Parents group told her story: "A nosy woman kept asking why, at my age, we hadn't provided a sibling for our daughter. At first I felt embarrassed. Finally, I said she had had a brother but he died at three months. The woman realized what she'd done, turned red, apologized, and walked out of the store!" Next time, the questioner was probably much more sensitive!

In an attempt to find some explanation for your child's death, people may offer too quickly or simplistically, "God must have had a reason for this." A reason—beyond our understanding—might exist, but this sheds no light on what happened, nor does this bring as much comfort as we like to feel. One wise father answered similar comments this way: "Yes, I'm sure God has a reason. But he hasn't told us what it is, and I sure miss my boy a lot."

More sensitive people may preface a question or comment by saying, "I don't want to hurt your feelings." Many misguided people think it an act of kindness to avoid mentioning your child or the death. Saying "It hurts more to *not* talk about my daughter" lets people know you're not afraid of the topic, and gives them permission to talk to you.

"Aren't you over it yet?" is usually asked by people who are afraid to deal with the reality of death. It is an insensitive question, and implies there is something wrong with you. Your response should be free of any guilt feelings. "No, I'm not over it yet, and I probably never will be. My heart is broken, and there are scars I will carry all my life. I am getting better, though—and part of a healthy recovery is talking about my child!"

"If only you'd had more faith" can cut deeply. Often this remark is made by people whose own faith is threatened by your experience. There are several ways to answer. "I believe God did his will, and I accept it" affirms your faith in God and your maturity in facing reality. "A lack of faith didn't end my son's life. It was a lack of self-control in an alcoholic driver," points out that life is a complex weaving of factors. "I don't use my faith as a way to manipulate God. I will trust him no matter what problems I face" may be the best response of all.

"But—you have *other* children!" Our children don't come in groups; they are individuals. While the remaining children can be a source of comfort, strength, and joy, they can never replace the child who died. Each child is unique, leaving a special imprint on our hearts and lives. "Yes, I'm glad for my kids; but Matthew was Matthew, and I'll always miss him" makes the point.

Some of the comments you hear will hurt. They will show how little people know of your experience. Try to be patient. Your friends love you and just don't have words to say what they feel. "A word fitly spoken" can silence busybodies, correct wrong assumptions, and open the door for meaningful discussion.

Sometimes friends don't visit as often as they once did. They haven't forgotten you. As one man put it, "I don't know what to say to Jim and Ann, so rather than say the wrong thing, I just say nothing." Reminding friends that you *like* to have your child remembered can set them at ease. Real friends won't stay away long.

There are some people who can't cope with the reality of death, so they do avoid you. Don't take offense at their immaturity. Your strength may challenge them to change.

Twenty-three

A New Beginning

Behold, I make all things new
(Rev. 21:5a).

His compassions fail not.
They are new every morning:
great is thy faithfulness
(Lam. 3:22b–23).

*M*aybe you don't feel like it now, but some day you'll be ready to start living again. That day cannot be rushed but it *will* come.

When your child died, so did a part of you. Your world stopped. You did the things that had to be done. You went through the appropriate social motions. Then all the activity stopped. You cared for the follow-up decisions with insurance companies, hospitals, and the funeral home.

Your friends and relatives went home after the funeral and seem to have gone back to normal. But there's no "normal" for you. It's a struggle to get up and get through the day. Dealing with people is exhausting. But you're doing it with help.

God's response to death is always life. That doesn't mean he gives another child when one dies. It means that out of the sorrow and ruin of your "other" life, God gives you a new life. It grows on you slowly, as you work through your grief. God gives you "beauty for ashes, the oil of joy for mourning" (Isa. 61:3).

One sign of making a new beginning is the ability to laugh. Often laughter is thought inappropriate—even a sin—in time of sorrow. Memories will prompt smiles. It's okay—and good—to be able to laugh about what was funny. It's also important to be able to laugh at yourself.

Another sign of a new beginning is not worrying about what to say to people when they ask questions. After Don died, Kaye was uncertain what to say when new people asked how many children she had. She answered: "I have four kids at home, and one son in heaven." That response tells people she's experienced a death in the family, but also affirms her willingness to talk about it.

A sure sign of a new beginning is your desire and ability to help others who are grieving. When you have experienced God's comfort, you want to share it. "Blessed be God, . . . the God of all comfort, who comforts us in our tribulation, that we may be able to comfort others who are in trouble with the same comfort we received from God (2 Cor. 1:3–4, paraphrased). When you are ready to *give*, the healing is almost complete.

Some years after his daughter's death, Tom was let go from his job. His severance package included tuition costs for retraining. Tom went back to school to learn how to be a grief counselor. His goal was to take what he'd learned from Tarah's death and use it to help other bereaved parents. This proved to be the right decision for him. It was Tom's new beginning.

For Further Reading

Bayly, Joseph. *The Last Thing We Talk About.* Elgin, Ill.: David C. Cook Publishing Company, 1969.

Grotenhuis, Eleanor. *Song of Triumph.* Grand Rapids: Baker Book House, 1991.

Kuhlman, Edward. *An Overwhelming Interference.* Old Tappan, N.J.: Fleming H. Revell Company, 1986.

Schiff, Harriet Sarnoff. *The Bereaved Parent.* New York: Crown Publishing, 1987.

Speiss, Margaret. *Cries from the Heart.* Grand Rapids: Baker Book House, 1991.

Westberg, Granger E. *Good Grief.* Philadelphia: Fortress Press, 1971.

Wolterstorff, Nicholas. *Lament for a Son.* Grand Rapids: Wm. B. Eerdmans Publishing Company, 1987.

Support Groups for Bereaved Parents

The Compassionate Friends
P.O. Box 3696
Oakbrook, IL 60521
(708) 990-0100

Brothers And Sisters In Support (BASIS)
237 Fairfield Avenue
Upper Darby, PA 19082
(215) 352-7177

MADD—Mothers Against Drunk Driving
669 Airport Freeway
Hurst, TX 76053

SIDS Alliance (Sudden Infant Death Syndrome)
10500 Little Patuxent Parkway
Suite 420
Columbia, MD 21044
1-800-221-SIDS

SHARE
St. Joseph's Health Center
300 First Capital Street
St. Charles, MO 63301
(314) 947-5000
For parents suffering a miscarriage, stillbirth, or other birth complications.

Churches and hospitals often sponsor grief support groups.

Many newspapers carry a weekly listing of area support groups.